Twenty Little Amish Quilts

With Full-Size Templates

Gwen Marston

Illustrations by Pat Holly

DOVER PUBLICATIONS, INC.

New York

Acknowledgments

All quilts designed and made by Gwen Marston
All illustrations by Pat Holly
Photographs by The Keva Partnership
Thanks to Ann Augustin for proofreading
Log Cabin quilt owned by Cindy Gillespie

Thanks for the support of my many quilting friends
to whom this book is dedicated.

Other Books by the Author

With the exception of *Q is for Quilt,* all books are co-authored by
Joe Cunningham.

American Beauties: Rose and Tulip Quilts, American Quilters
   Society, Paducah, Kentucky, 1988.
Amish Quilting Patterns. Dover Publications, Inc., New York, 1987.
Mary Schafer and Her Quilts. Michigan State University Press,
   East Lansing, Michigan, 1990.
Q is for Quilt. Michigan State University Press, 1987.
Quilting with Style: Principles for Great Pattern Design,
   American Quilters Society, 1993.
Sets and Borders. American Quilters Society, 1987.
70 Classic Quilting Patterns. Dover Publications, Inc., 1987.
Twenty Little Patchwork Quilts. Dover Publications, Inc., 1990.

Copyright © 1993 by Gwen Marston.
All rights reserved under Pan American and International Copyright Conventions.

Published in Canada by General Publishing Company, Ltd., 30 Lesmill Road, Don Mills, Toronto, Ontario.
Published in the United Kingdom by Constable and Company, Ltd., 3 The Lanchesters, 162–164 Fulham Palace Road, London W6 9ER.

Twenty Little Amish Quilts: With Full-Size Templates is a new work, first published by Dover Publications, Inc. in 1993.

Manufactured in the United States of America
Dover Publications, Inc., 31 East 2nd Street, Mineola, N.Y. 11501

Library of Congress Cataloging-in-Publication Data

Marston, Gwen.
   Twenty little Amish quilts : with full-size templates / Gwen Marston ; illustrations by Pat Holly.
       p.   cm. — (Dover needlework series)
    ISBN 0-486-27582-5 (pbk.)
    1. Patchwork—Patterns.   2. Doll quilts, Amish.   I. Title.   II. Series.
TT835.M3782   1993
746.9′7041—dc20   93-9357
                                                                      CIP

Introduction

Rich saturated color, simple pieced designs and beautiful quilting patterns are what first attracted me to Amish quilts. I began my adventures by making a series of full-size quilts in the styles of both Old Order Lancaster County and Midwest Amish antique quilts. More recently, I enjoyed making this collection of Amish doll quilts. In retrospect, it might have been wiser to begin with small quilts and work my way up to the more ambitious projects since making small quilts is a good way to discover the characteristics that make Amish quilts unique.

Early Amish doll quilts were scaled-down and simplified versions of full-size bed quilts. The quilts were almost exclusively made of solid rich colors and the quilting designs were most often worked with dark thread.

The construction of many antique Amish doll quilts is quite primitive, suggesting that they were made by children learning to sew. Sewing was a valuable skill that many mothers felt obliged to pass on to their daughters. Such instruction was no doubt more successful when little girls were tempted by making a quilt for their dollies.

In making this collection of twenty small Amish quilts, I tried to capture the essence of the Amish design tradition. They are all quick and easy to make. Experimenting with color was one of the most enjoyable aspects of making these quilts for me and I encourage you to do the same.

Instructions

Quiltmaking employs a number of techniques: making templates, cutting fabric, sewing pieces together, quilting and finishing the edges. None of these steps are particularly complicated, and anyone with sewing experience can learn quiltmaking easily. Here are a few ideas to guide you along, but remember that there are no hard and fast rules. If you need more information, your local library will have a section of instructional quilt books. Quilt shops also carry a growing number of books, quilt magazines and videos which provide basic instruction.

Fabric

Early Amish quilts were made of wool, cotton or rayon. The quilts in this book were made with cotton and occasionally small amounts of cotton sateen. Sateen has a sheen to it which can add texture and interest. I choose a wide assortment of predominantly dark colors to work with. I often use a slightly different tone of a color already being used to add interest.

Because of the small scale of these quilts I do not include yardage requirements in the directions. These small quilts can be made with small amounts of fabric and scraps. The only large piece of fabric needed is for the backing, and three quarters of a yard of fabric is adequate for any of the quilts in this book.

It is a good idea to wash and iron all of your fabrics before you use them to make sure they are pre-shrunk and that the colors do not run. For the small amounts you will need for these quilts it is easy to hand wash them in a sink. That way you can easily see if the fabrics are color safe. Once the fabric is washed and dried, cut off the selvage and press the fabric flat, so it will be easy to work with.

Templates

Templates are the pattern pieces you will use to cut the patches that make up the quilt blocks. Accurate templates will help ensure accurate piecing—and the smaller the patches the more important accuracy becomes. The pattern pieces used to make these quilts are printed on lightweight cardboard in the center of the book. If you piece by hand you can simply cut out the templates and use them as they are. If you piece on the sewing machine, you must add ¼″ seam allowance around each pattern piece before cutting it out. We have left room between the templates for you to do this.

To make your templates even more durable, glue the pages to another sheet of lightweight cardboard before cutting, or trace the templates onto translucent plastic.

Marking and Cutting the Patches

Each pattern piece has an arrow on it, indicating which side to lay on the straight of the grain of the fabric. Following these when you cut the patches will make sure that the outside edges of the blocks will be on the straight of the grain. Keeping all of the outside edges of the block on the straight of the grain will help keep your quilt square as you work.

Before you cut all the pieces for your quilt, it is a good idea to make a sample block to make sure your templates are accurate.

Draw around each template on the wrong side of your fabric with a sharp pencil. A regular lead pencil works for most marking. For dark fabrics I use a white or silver Berol Verithin pencil, available at most art or drafting supply shops, as well as many quilt stores.

When tracing pieces for hand-sewing, remember that you are marking the *sewing* line on the fabric, not the cutting line. You must leave a ¼″ margin around these pieces when you cut. For machine-piecing, cut on your traced line.

I find I can precisely cut up to four layers of fabric at once. That means I only have to mark the top layer. Make sure the layers are pressed flat and that you have good, sharp scissors to work with. Accurate cutting is especially important for machine-sewing, as you will be following the edge of the fabric to guide your sewing line.

Sewing

I pieced the blocks for all these quilts on the machine. Of course, they could be done by hand, but these instructions are for machine sewing. Use dark thread when sewing on dark fabrics.

Set the stitch length at 10 or 12 stitches to the inch. Sew the patches together with a ¼″ seam allowance. It is not necessary to backstitch because you will be sewing over all the seams in another direction. The only place you need to backstitch is on the seams of the outside borders, which can pull apart when the top is stretched for quilting.

Sewing any quilt block together involves starting with small units that can be joined together into larger units. To make a black and green Four Patch block for instance, first sew one black square to one green square, repeat, then join the two units to make the complete block. Nearly all quilt blocks can be divided into small units like this, which can then be assembled along straight seams.

Mass sewing, or "chain piecing," will make your work go faster. For example, to make many Four Patch blocks, begin by sewing all the black squares to the green ones, one after another, without lifting the presser foot or cutting the thread between the pairs of patches. Once you have sewn them all, clip them apart. (If you are sewing triangles, trim the protruding points so they won't get in your way when you are quilting.) Now press the seams to one side before you continue.

Once the blocks are done, sew them into rows of blocks. If you are using lattice strips between the blocks, sew them to the blocks first. Finally, pin the rows of blocks together, pinning the junctions where the points will meet carefully, then sew them together to complete the top. All the borders for these quilts were made by first pinning and sewing on the side borders, then repeating the process for the top and bottom borders.

Quilting Designs

These small quilts don't leave much room for elaborate quilting designs. Amish quilters typically criss-crossed square patches from corner to corner. The narrow borders require simple, small-scale designs. A good reference for Amish quilting designs is *Amish Quilting Patterns* by Joe Cunningham and me, also published by Dover Publications (ISBN 0-486-25326-0).

Most of these quilts are made with dark fabrics, so I like to use a white or silver Berol Verithin pencil to mark the quilting designs. They are easy to use and wash out completely.

Quilting patterns can be traced directly onto light fabrics, and with the aid of a light table, onto dark fabrics as well. In some cases it is easier to make a cardboard template to draw around.

Backing

Cut the back of your quilt 1″ to 1½″ larger all around than the top. You can choose one of the fabrics from your quilt top, or introduce an entirely new fabric for the back of your quilt.

Batting

I prefer to use a thin cotton batting in small quilts. Polyester batting seems too puffy for these small quilts and the fibers can migrate through the surface of your quilt and "pill" or "beard." On dark fabrics the bearding is obvious, and that is the main reason I recommend using a cotton batt for quilts made with dark solid fabrics. There are a number of different brands on the market. I suggest trying a few out to see which one you like best.

Quilting

These small quilts can be easily quilted in your lap, in a hoop or in a full-size frame. If you lap quilt or use a hoop, you will need to baste the three layers together.

I think I get the best results from stretching the quilt in a full-size frame, which I make myself. It is simply four 1″ × 2″ pine boards about 36″ long. To each board, I staple a length of sturdy fabric which sticks out about ½″ over the long edge of the board. Baste the edges of the back to two of the boards, lay these across the other two boards and secure them with small C-clamps. Pin the two loose edges of the quilt back to the fabric strips every 1″ to 2″. Spread the batting over the backing and smooth it out. Lay the quilt top on the batting and pin around the edges through all layers. Check to make sure it is stretched tightly and that there are no wrinkles in the backing or the top, and you are ready to begin quilting.

The Quilting Stitch

From my own experience, I know it is easier to learn to quilt by watching someone than by reading instructions, but here are some tips to get you started. The stitch is nothing more than a running stitch—but it is done differently than other hand-sewing. Short needles called "betweens" are made for just this purpose. The larger the number, the smaller the needle. I use a number 9, but quilters vary a great deal on the size of the needle they like to use. Cotton quilting thread will knot and ravel less than polyester thread. I use a regular nickel silver thimble to guide the needle through the quilt.

There are two ways to begin quilting that I use. One way is to begin with a knot at the end of a 14″ to 16″ length of thread. Insert the needle about ½″ away from where you want to begin quilting and bring the needle out at that point. Now tug lightly on the knot and pop it through

4

the surface and into the middle of the quilt. A second way is the "no knot" method. Start with twice the length of thread you would normally use. Begin quilting, leaving half of the thread lying loose on the quilt top. Once you have completed one line of quilting, simply thread the loose end into the needle and continue quilting with the other half of the thread.

Place your thimble on the middle finger of your right hand. The thimble will guide the needle through the fabric on top of the quilt, while the fingers of the left hand are placed underneath the quilt to feel the needle as it comes through. The finger below the quilt should be pushing up enough to create a ridge on the surface, enabling you to determine exactly where to aim the point of the needle. As the needle slips through and touches the finger below, rock the needle down with your thimble and push in to the surface, repeating this motion until you have three or four stitches on the needle. Then pull the thread through. Try to make the stitches even. With practice, your stitches will become smaller and more even. If you continue to have trouble with the quilting stitch, find a quilter to work with you for awhile.

To end the quilting line, slip the needle between the layers and bring it back to the surface about 1″ away. Try to bring it up in a seam, but if none is handy, bring it up in a quilting line. Repeat this twice in one direction and once in reverse. Pull the needle through, hold it taut and clip the thread close to the quilt top so that the end will bounce back inside. Now the end of the thread is woven around inside the quilt and won't come out.

Binding

Many Amish quilts were bound by simply bringing the backing around to the top and top-stitching it. I set the stitch length to 12 to 15 stitches to the inch for a neat, tiny stitch. Trim the batting even with the edge of the top. Trim the backing so it extends beyond the edges of the top by ½″. Fold the backing around to the top, turn the edge under ¼″ and sew along the edge. Work carefully and slowly for the neatest job. A typical way Midwest Amish quilters secure the corner is to stitch to the very edge of one side and sew a little triangle as you turn the corner (Fig 1).

Old Order Lancaster Amish Quilts most often used a wide separate binding, cut on the straight grain. For these small quilts a finished ½″ binding works well. Cut the binding 1½″ wide to include the seam allowance. Cut the strips on the cross grain because it has more give to it than the straight grain. Straight grain is lengthwise, parallel to the selvage; cross grain is perpendicular to the selvage.

Add the binding to the two opposite sides first. Lay the binding along the edge of the top side of your quilt, right sides together and sew in place. For ½″ binding, trim the batting and backing ½″ outside the seam line (for ¼″ binding, trim all three layers evenly). Bring the binding

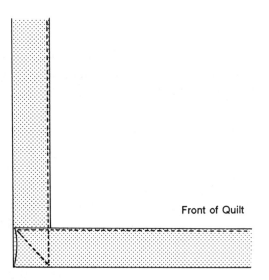

Fig. 1

Machine stitching is on the front of the quilt. The back is brought around to the top.

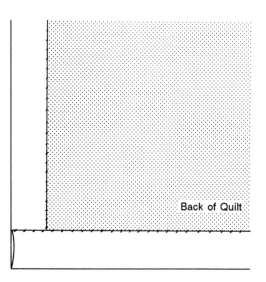

Fig. 2

A separate binding is hand stitched on the back of the quilt.

around to the back, fold under the seam allowance and sew it down with a hidden stitch. Add the other two borders in the same way, leaving ½″ free at both ends. Fold the raw edges under, bring the binding around to the back and stitch in place (Fig 2).

Finishing the binding is always a wonderful feeling because it means you can begin your next little Amish quilt.

One Patch with Corner Blocks

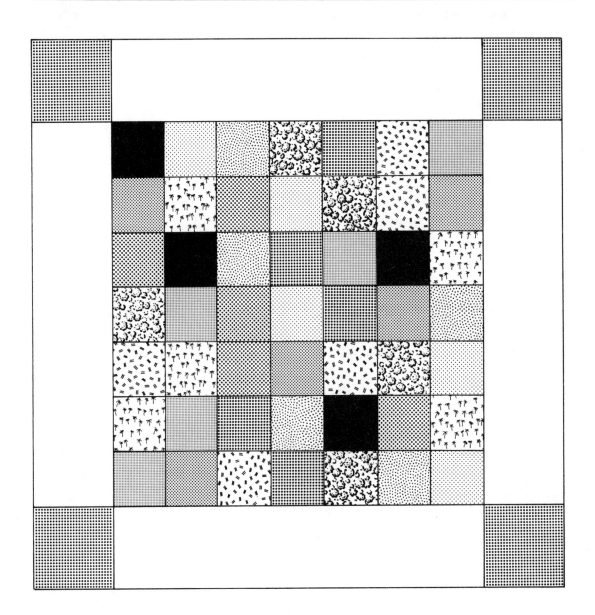

Templates to use: E

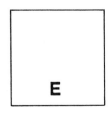

One Patch with Corner Blocks

Finished Size:
Quilt - 21" x 21"
($^1/_2$" binding)

Number of pieces to cut:

E - 49 random colors

Borders:
Finished size is 3" x 14"
Cut 4 - $3^1/_2$" x $14^1/_2$"

Corner squares:
Finished size is 3" square
Cut 4 - $3^1/_2$" square

To Assemble:

Lay out the 49 squares (7 across, 7 down) to determine color placement. Sew seven squares E together to make a row (Fig. 1). Repeat to make seven rows. Sew rows together, making sure squares line up.

Add side borders. Sew a corner square to both ends of two borders. Add to top and bottom. Finish the quilt following the General Instructions.

E

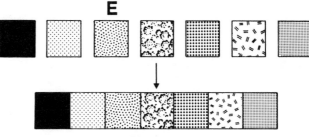

Fig. 1

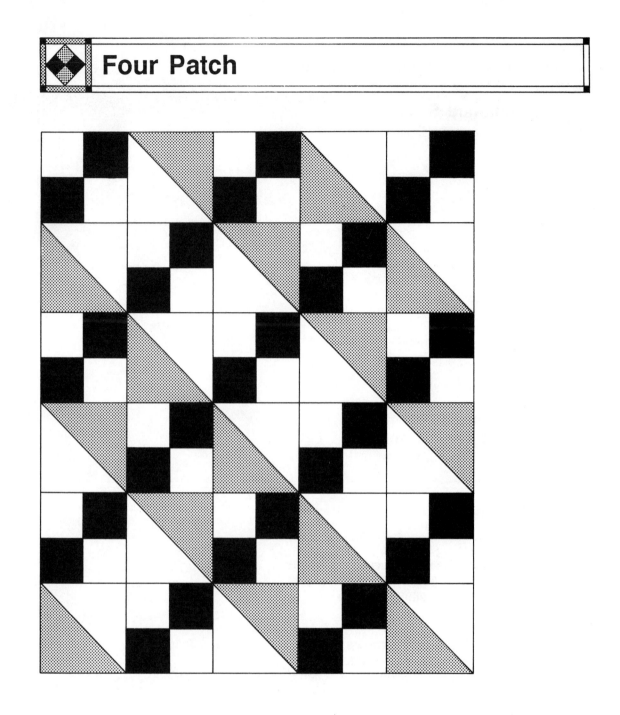

Four Patch

Templates to use: A, B

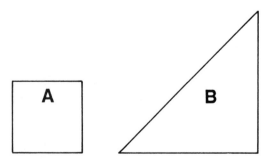

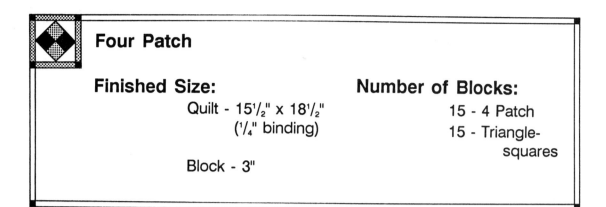

Four Patch

Finished Size:
Quilt - 15½" x 18½"
(¼" binding)

Block - 3"

Number of Blocks:
15 - 4 Patch
15 - Triangle-
squares

Number of pieces to cut:

A - 30 light, 30 dark
B - 15 light, 15 dark

To Assemble:

Make blocks first:
4 Patch block - Sew a light square A to a dark square A (Fig. 1). Repeat. Press seams towards dark fabric. Arrange the 2 rows as in Fig. 2. Sew these two rows together. Repeat to make 15 blocks.

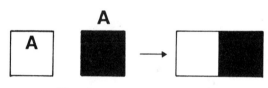

Fig. 1

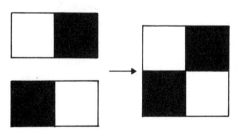

Fig. 2

Triangle-squares - Sew a light triangle B to a dark triangle B (Fig. 3). Repeat to make 15 blocks.

Sew A and B blocks into rows - Lay out all 30 blocks using the drawing as a guide. Make sure the blocks are arranged to form the diagonal pattern. Sew blocks together to make six rows. Sew rows together. Finish the quilt following the General Instructions.

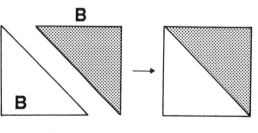

Fig. 3

Four Patch with Lattice

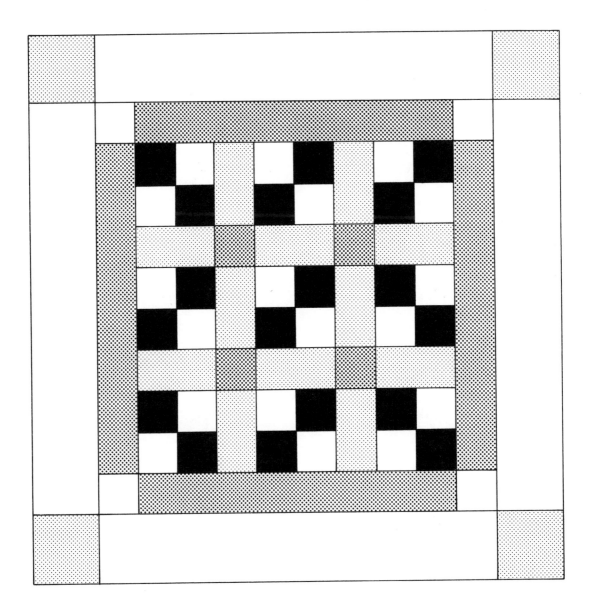

Templates to use: A, Q

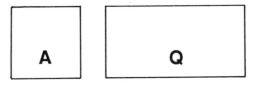

A   Q

10

Four Patch with Lattice

Finished Size:
Quilt - 20" x 20"
(¹/₂" binding)

Block - 3"

Number of Blocks: 9

Number of pieces to cut:

For each block: **Total:**

A   2 light, 2 dark   18 light, 18 dark

Lattice: A - 4
            Q - 12

Borders:
Inner   Finished size is 1¹/₂" x 12"
        Cut 4 - 2" x 12¹/₂"

        Corners:
        Cut 4 using Template A

Outer   Finished size is 2¹/₂" x 15"
        Cut 4 - 3" x 15¹/₂"

        Corners:
        Finished size is 2¹/₂" square
        Cut 4 - 3" squares

To Assemble:

Construct inner area first. Sew one light square A to one dark square A (Fig. 1). Repeat.

Sew these units together, alternating light and dark (Fig. 2). Repeat to make nine 4 Patch blocks.

Make rows with the 4 Patch blocks alternating with rectangle Q, using three blocks and two rectangles (Fig. 3). Repeat to make three rows.

Make lattice row by alternating three rectangles Q with two squares A (Fig. 4). Repeat to make two rows.

Sew rows together, alternating 4 Patch rows with lattice rows.

Add inner side borders. Sew corner squares A to ends on inner top and bottom borders. Sew these units to the top and bottom. Add outer side borders. Sew corner squares to ends of outer top and bottom borders. Add these units to the top and bottom. Finish quilt following the General Instructions.

Fig. 1

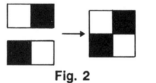

Fig. 2

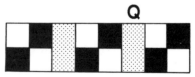

Fig. 3

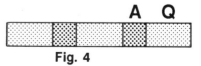

Fig. 4

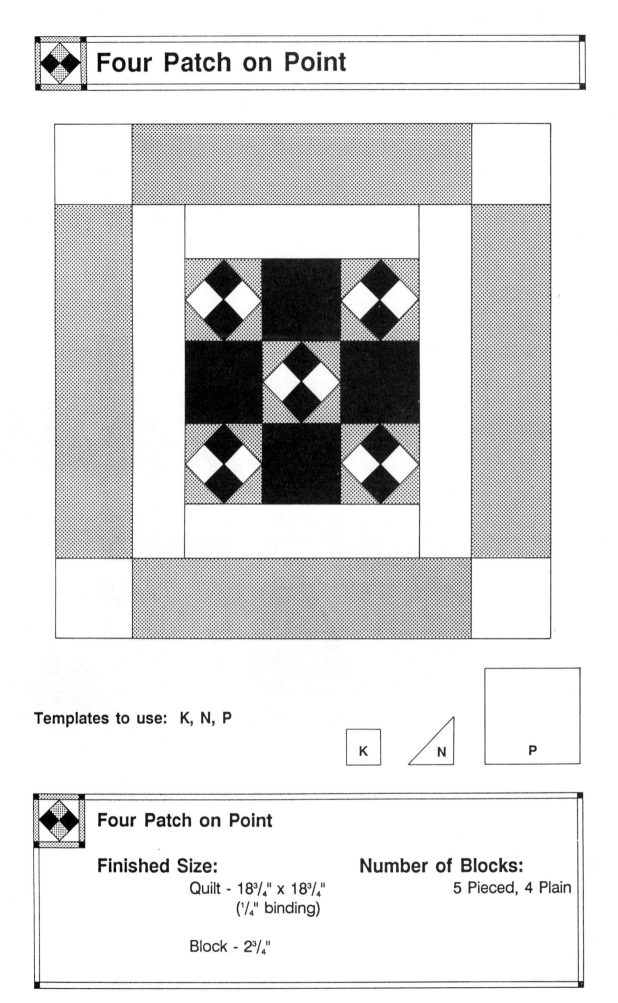

Templates to use: K, N, P

K

N

P

Four Patch on Point

Finished Size:
Quilt - $18^3/_4$" x $18^3/_4$"
($^1/_4$" binding)

Block - $2^3/_4$"

Number of Blocks:
5 Pieced, 4 Plain

Number of pieces to cut:

Pieced block:

	For each block:	Total:
K	2 light, 2 dark	10 light, 10 dark
N	4 medium	20 medium

Plain blocks:
    P - 4 dark

Borders:

Inner   Side
        Finished size is 2" x 8¼"
        Cut 2 - 2½" x 8¾"

        Top & Bottom
        Finished size is 2" x 12¼"
        Cut 2 - 2½" x 12¾"

Outer   Finished size is 3" x 12¼"
        Cut 4 - 3½" x 12¾"

        Corner squares
        Finished size is 3" square
        Cut 4 - 3½" squares

To Assemble:

Make the inner portion first. Sew one light K and one dark K together (Fig. 1). Repeat.

Fig. 1

Sew these two units together so the dark and light squares alternate (Fig. 2).

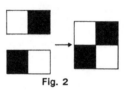

Fig. 2

Sew four triangles N to the sides of this 4 patch block (Fig. 3). Repeat to make five blocks.

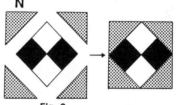

Fig. 3

Lay out Pieced blocks and Plain blocks. Make two rows with two 4 Patch blocks and one Plain block (Fig. 4).

Fig. 4

Make one row with one 4 Patch block and two Plain blocks (Fig. 5).

Sew blocks together to make rows.

Sew rows together. Add side inner borders, then top and bottom inner borders.

Sew outer borders to sides. Sew corner squares to the other two outer borders. Sew these units to the top and bottom. Finish the quilt following the General Instructions.

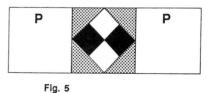

Fig. 5

Zig Zag

Templates to use: C, D

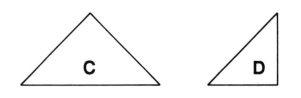

Zig Zag

Finished Size:
Quilt - 17" x 20"
($\frac{1}{4}$" binding)

Number of Rows: 11

Number of pieces to cut:

C - 66 light, 66 dark
D - 11 light, 11 dark

If you want each zig zag row to be different, you will need eleven different colors. Cut 12 C and 2 D of each color. Using the drawing and photo as a guide, lay out the rows.

To Assemble:

This quilt will be assembled in eleven vertical strips. Each strip begins and ends with a triangle D. The 12 triangles C will alternate light and dark. The strip next to it will have the light and dark triangles in reverse position. It helps to lay out all the pieces to be sure you get the zig zag effect.

To sew each strip, start at the top with a triangle D and sew to a triangle C. Add the next triangle C and so on until twelve triangles C have been sewn together. Sew the final triangle D at the bottom (Fig. 1).

After the vertical strips are assembled, sew the strips together. Mark the midpoint of the long edge of the triangle C. This will line up with the point of the triangle in the neighboring strip (Fig. 1).

Finish the quilt following the General Instructions.

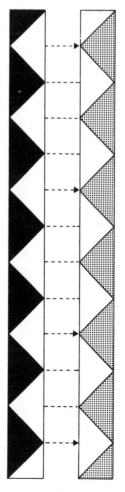

Fig. 1

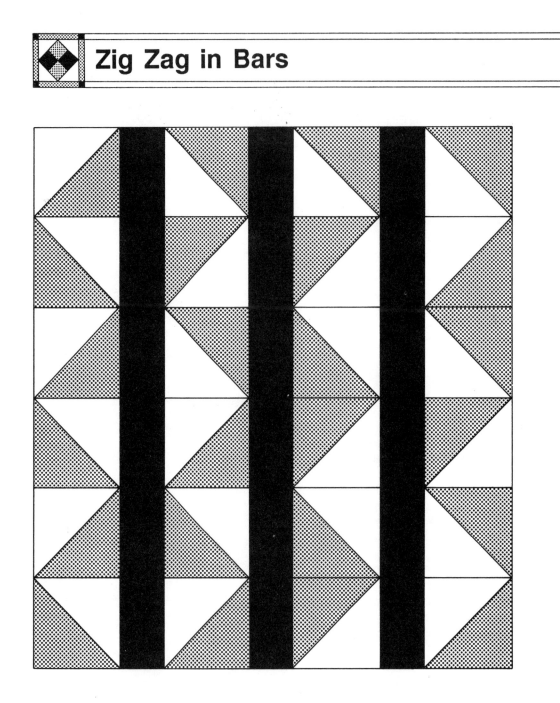

Templates to use: B

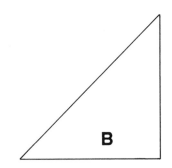

Zig Zag in Bars

Finished Size: **Number of Blocks: 24**

Quilt - 17" x 18$\frac{1}{2}$"
($\frac{1}{4}$" binding)

Block - 3"

Number of pieces to cut:

B -   24 light, 24 dark
(both varied)

Vertical Lattice Bars -
Finished bars are 1$\frac{1}{2}$" x 18".
Cut 3 - 2" x 18$\frac{1}{2}$" dark

To Assemble:

To make blocks, sew a light triangle B to a dark triangle B (Fig. 1). Repeat to make 24 blocks.

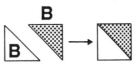

Fig. 1

Lay out blocks and strips. See photo for one way to arrange. Sew six blocks together to make one vertical row (Fig. 2). Repeat for other three rows.

Sew rows and bars together - mark midpoint of bar (see Fig. 2), match this with the center of block row and sew. Repeat with the remaining rows and bars.

Finish the quilt following the General Instructions.

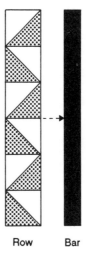

Row   Bar

Fig. 2

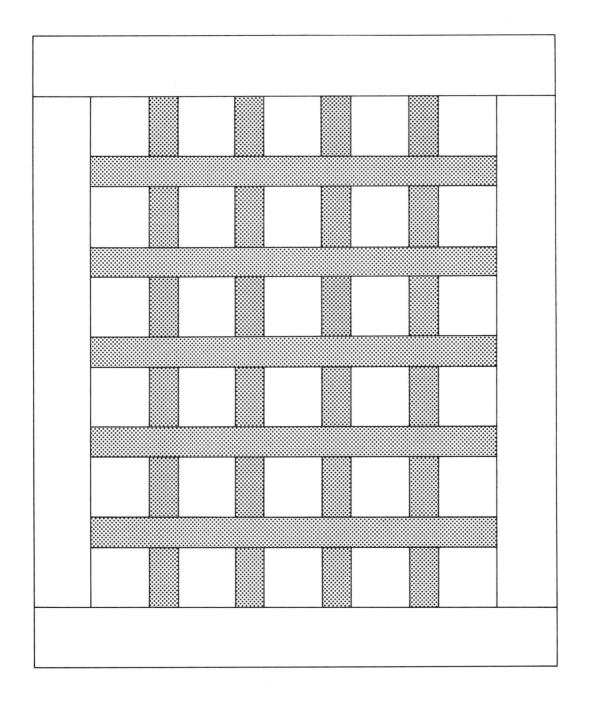

Templates to use: E, F

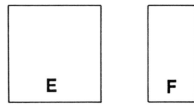

Squares in Bars

Finished Size:
Quilt - 18$\frac{1}{2}$" x 21$\frac{1}{2}$"
($\frac{1}{4}$" binding)

Number of pieces to cut:

E - 30 (varied)
F - 24 (varied)

Lattice strips:
Finished size is 1" x 14"
Cut 5 strips 1$\frac{1}{2}$" x 14$\frac{1}{2}$"

Borders:
Sides:
Finished size is 2" x 17"
Cut 2 - 2$\frac{1}{2}$" x 17$\frac{1}{2}$"

Top & Bottom:
Finished size is 2" x 18"
Cut 2 - 2$\frac{1}{2}$" x 18$\frac{1}{2}$"

To Assemble:

Sew the long side of rectangle F to a square E (Fig. 1).

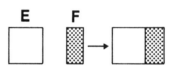

Fig. 1

Add a square E to the other long side of F (Fig. 2).

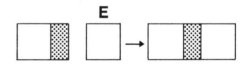

Fig. 2

Add another F to the square E; continue until you have sewn five squares and four rectangles (Fig. 3). Repeat to make six rows of squares and rectangles.

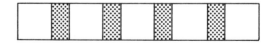

Fig. 3

Lay out the pieced rows and alternate these with the lattice bars. Sew rows and bars together. Add side borders, then top and bottom borders.

Finish the quilt following the General Instructions.

Sunshine and Shadow

Templates to use: A

A

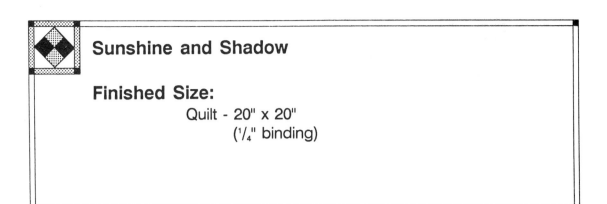

Sunshine and Shadow

Finished Size:
Quilt - 20" x 20"
($^1/_4$" binding)

Number of pieces to cut:

This quilt gets its design from the placement of colors in the squares. You can use different colors in the "rounds". Each round can be different or you may repeat colors.

Round	Cut from Template A
1	1
2	4
3	8
4	12
5	16
6	16
7	12
8	8
9	4

Borders:
Finished size is 3" x 13$^1/_2$"
Cut 4 - 3$^1/_2$" x 14"

Corner Squares:
Finished size is 3" x 3"
Cut 4 - 3$^1/_2$" x 3$^1/_2$"

To Assemble:

Following the diagram, lay out the squares A in the "rounds". Assemble by sewing Row 1 across, then Row 2, until all rows are sewn together. Attach Row 1 to Row 2, Row 1-2 to Row 3, Row 1-2-3 to Row 4 and so on. Add side borders. Sew corner squares to the other borders and sew these to the top and bottom. Finish the quilt following the General Instructions.

9	8	7	6	5	6	7	8	9	Row 1
8	7	6	5	4	5	6	7	8	Row 2
7	6	5	4	3	4	5	6	7	Row 3
6	5	4	3	2	3	4	5	6	Row 4
5	4	3	2	1	2	3	4	5	Row 5
6	5	4	3	2	3	4	5	6	Row 6
7	6	5	4	3	4	5	6	7	Row 7
8	7	6	5	4	5	6	7	8	Row 8
9	8	7	6	5	6	7	8	9	Row 9

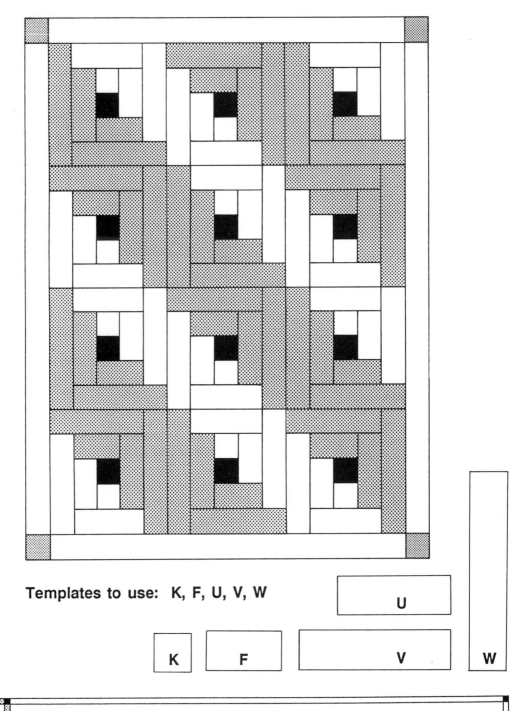

Templates to use: K, F, U, V, W

U

K   F   V   W

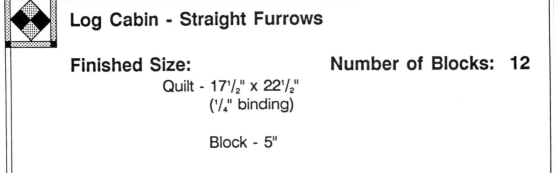

Log Cabin - Straight Furrows

Finished Size: **Number of Blocks: 12**

Quilt - 17$\frac{1}{2}$" x 22$\frac{1}{2}$"
($\frac{1}{4}$" binding)

Block - 5"

Number of pieces to cut:

For each block:		Total:
K	1 center	12 center
	1 light	12 light
F	1 light, 1 dark	12 light, 12 dark
U	1 light, 1 dark	12 light, 12 dark
V	1 light, 1 dark	12 light, 12 dark
W	1 dark	12 dark

Borders:

Top & Bottom
Finished size is 1" x 15"
Cut 2 - 1½" x 15½"

Sides
Finished size is 1" x 20"
Cut 2 - 1½" x 20½"

Corner squares
Cut 4 using template K

To Assemble:

Make blocks first. Start with center square K. Add a light K to one side (Fig. 1).

To the long side, add a light F. To the bottom, add a dark F (Fig. 2).

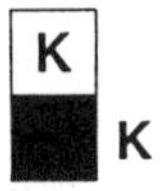

Fig. 1 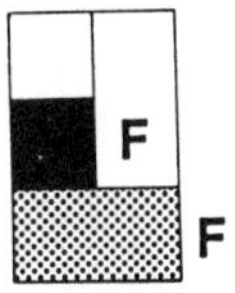   Fig. 2

Add a dark U to the left side. To the top, add a light U (Fig. 3).

To the right side, add a light V. To the bottom, add a dark V (Fig. 4).

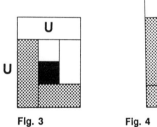
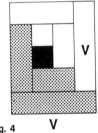

Fig. 3   Fig. 4   V

Add a dark W to the left side. Repeat to make 12 blocks (Fig. 5).

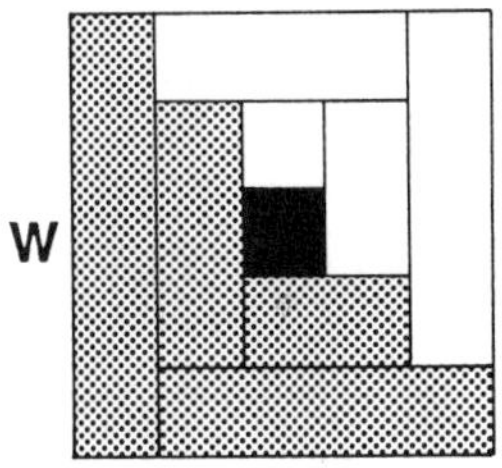

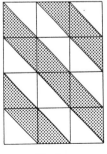

Fig. 5

Lay out the 12 blocks, three across, 4 down. Arrange the dark and light area of each block (Fig. 6). Sew blocks together to make rows, then sew rows together.

Add long borders to the sides. Sew a square K to both sides of the short borders. Add these to the top and bottom. Finish quilt following the General Instructions.

Fig. 6

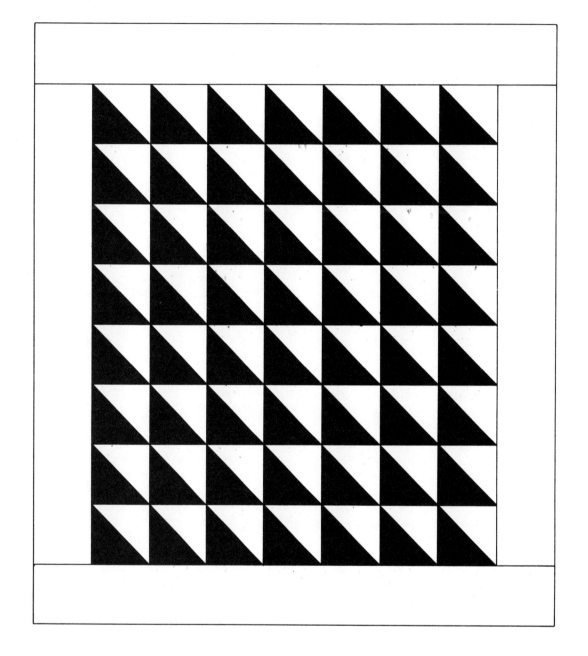

Templates to use: J

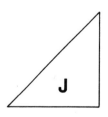

Add $^1/_4$" seam allowance around all edges.

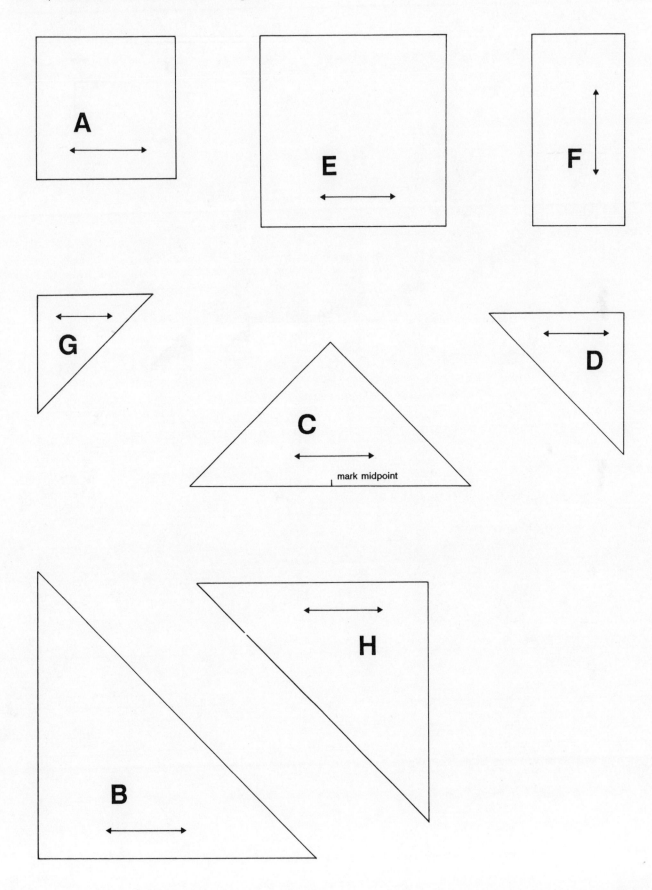

A

E

F

G

C

mark midpoint

D

H

B

PLATE 1

Add ¼" seam allowance around all edges.

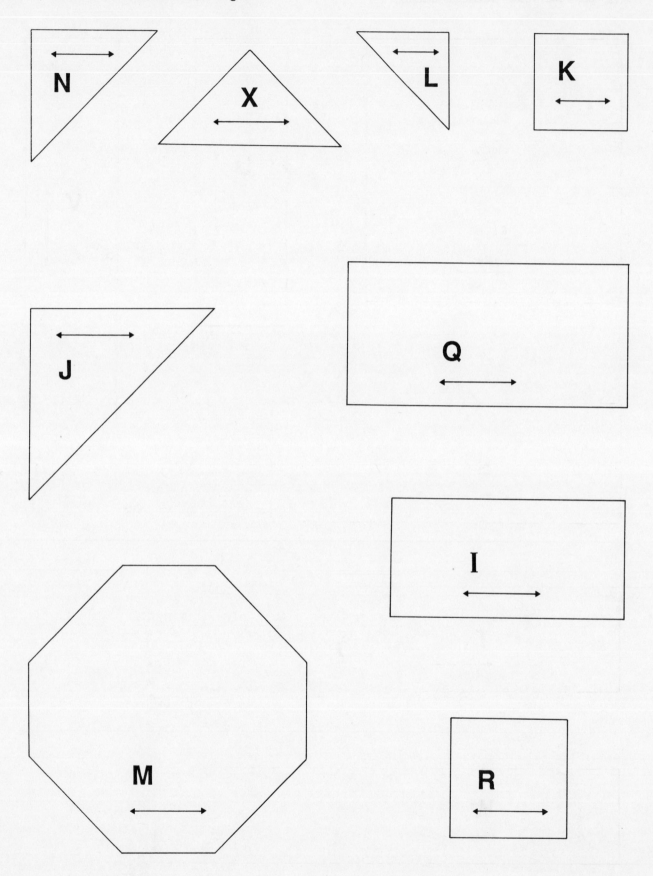

PLATE 2

Add ¹/₄" seam allowance around all edges.

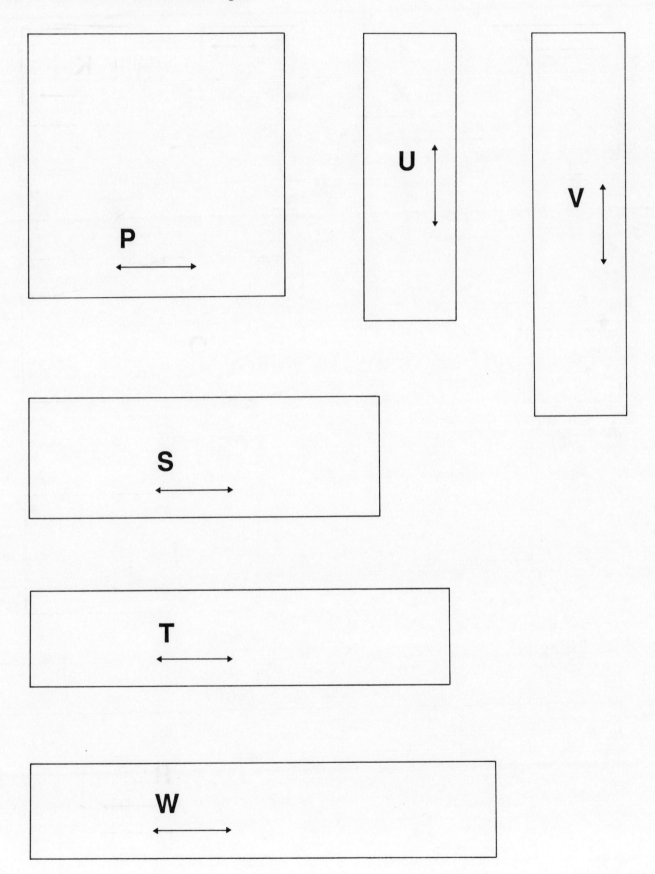

PLATE 3

Add $\frac{1}{4}$" seam allowance around all edges.

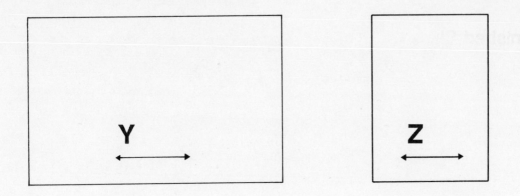

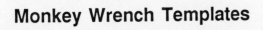

Monkey Wrench Templates

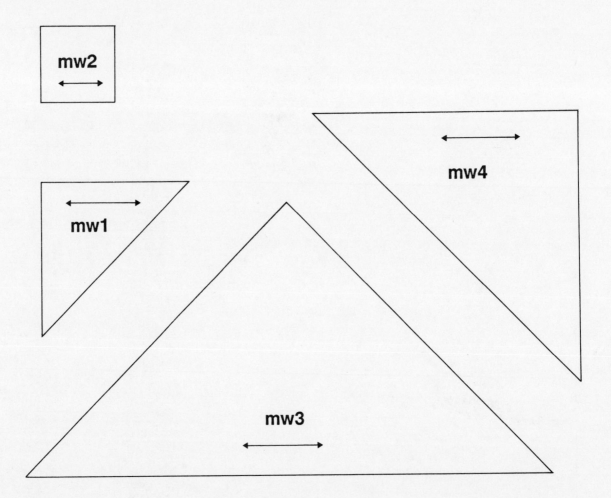

PLATE 4

Triangles

Finished Size:
> Quilt - 19" x 21"
> ($^1/_2$" binding)

Number of pieces to cut:

J - Cut 56 black, 56 assorted colors

See photo. The colors are arranged to form diagonal lines. If you choose to do this, count how many colored triangles are needed for each diagonal line.

Borders:
Side
Finished size is 2" x 16"
Cut 2 - 2$^1/_2$" x 16$^1/_2$"

Top & Bottom
Finished size is 2" x 18"
Cut 2 - 2$^1/_2$" x 18$^1/_2$"

To Assemble:

Sew triangles J together to form squares (Fig. 1).

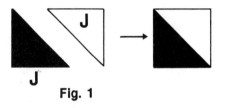

Fig. 1

Arrange squares as desired (eight rows of seven squares). Sew squares together to form rows (Fig. 2).

Fig. 2

Sew rows together. Add side borders, then top and bottom borders. Finish the quilt following the General Instructions.

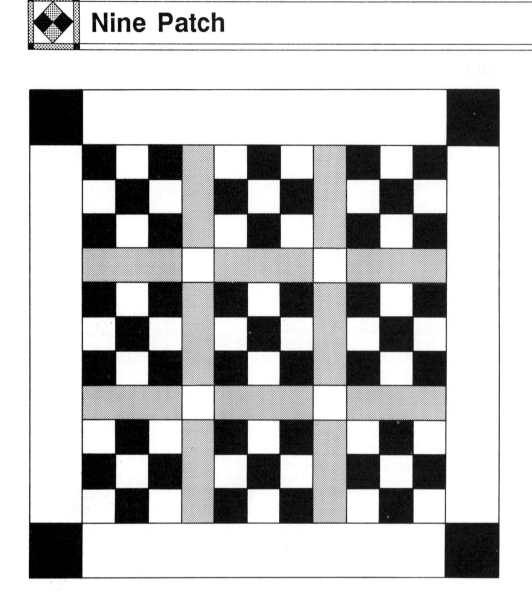

Templates to use: R, S

Nine Patch

Finished Size: **Number of Blocks:** 9

Quilt - 18³/₄" x 18³/₄"
(¹/₂" binding)

Block - 3³/₄"

Number of pieces to cut:

For each block: **Total:**   **Border:**

R   5 light, 4 dark or   81 light
    5 dark, 4 light   and dark

Lattice:
    R - 4
    S - 12

Border:
Finished size is 2" x 13³/₄"
Cut 4 - 2¹/₂" x 14¹/₄"

Corners:
Finished size is 2"
Cut 4 - 2¹/₂" squares

To Assemble:

Make 9 Patch blocks first. Arrange 5 light R and 4 dark R (or 5 dark R and 4 light R). Sew squares into three rows, sew rows together. Repeat to make nine blocks total (Fig. 1).

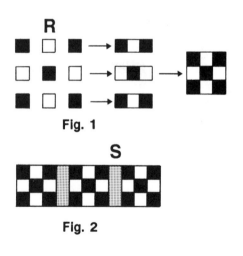

Fig. 1

Add lattice: Use three 9 Patch blocks and 2 rectangles S to form a row (Fig. 2). Sew together and repeat to make three rows.

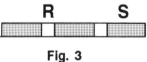

Fig. 2

Make lattice rows by sewing three rectangles S alternating with two squares R (Fig. 3). Make two lattice rows. Lay out 9 Patch rows alternating with lattice rows. Sew rows together.

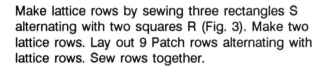

Fig. 3

Add side borders. Sew corner squares to top and bottom borders. Sew these units to top and bottom. Finish the quilt following the General Instructions.

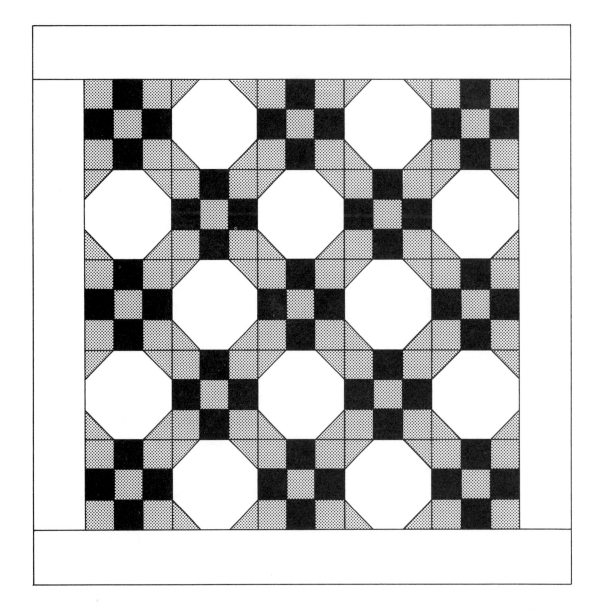

Templates to use: K, L, M

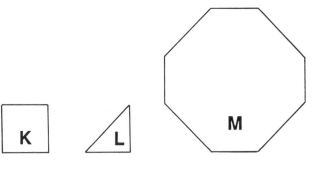

Nine Patch and Snowball

Finished Size:
Quilt - 19" x 19"
($\frac{1}{4}$" binding)

Block - 3"

Number of Blocks:
13 - 9 Patch
12 - Snowball

Number of pieces to cut:

9 Patch -	For each block:	Total:	Borders:
			Side
K	5 light	65 light	Finished size is 1 $\frac{3}{4}$" x 15
	4 dark	52 dark	Cut 2 - 2$\frac{1}{4}$" x 15$\frac{1}{2}$"
			Top & Bottom
Snowball -	For each block:	Total:	Finished size is 1 $\frac{3}{4}$" x 18$\frac{1}{2}$"
			Cut 2 - 2$\frac{1}{4}$" x 19"
L	4 color	48 color	
M	1 light	12 light	

To Assemble:

9 Patch -
Sew a "light" K to both sides of a "dark" K.
Repeat. Sew a "dark" K to both sides of a "light"
K. Sew rows together (Fig. 1). Make 13 blocks.

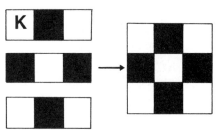

Fig. 1

Snowball -
Sew triangles L to corners of M (Fig. 2).
Make 12 blocks.

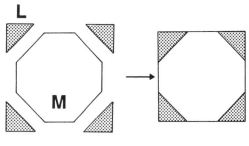

Fig. 2

Lay out blocks as in drawing, alternating 9 Patch
and Snowball blocks. Sew blocks together to
make five rows. Sew rows together. Add side
borders, then top and bottom borders.

Finish quilt following the General Instructions.

Evening Star

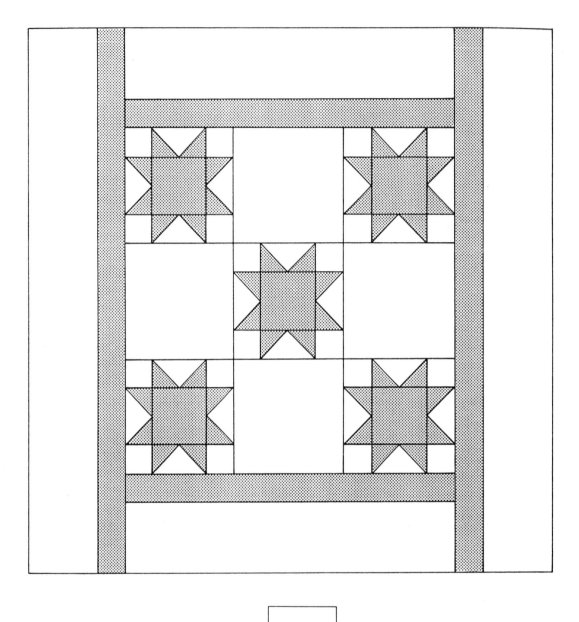

Templates to use: **E, K, L, X**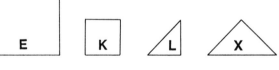

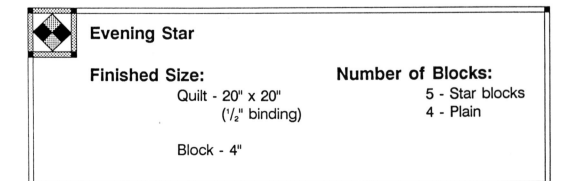

Evening Star

Finished Size:
Quilt - 20" x 20"
($^1/_2$" binding)

Block - 4"

Number of Blocks:
5 - Star blocks
4 - Plain

Number of pieces to cut:

For each block: **Total:**

E   1 star color   5
K   4 background   20
L   8 star color   40
X   4 background   20

Plain blocks:
     Finished size is 4" square.
     Cut 4 - 4$\frac{1}{2}$" square

Borders:

Inner   Top and bottom
         Finished size is 1" x 12"
         Cut 2 - 1$\frac{1}{2}$" x 12$\frac{1}{2}$"

         Sides
         Finished size is 1" x 19"
         Cut 2 - 1$\frac{1}{2}$" x 19$\frac{1}{2}$"

Outer   Top and bottom
         Finished size is 2$\frac{1}{2}$" x 12"
         Cut 2 - 3" x 12$\frac{1}{2}$"

         Sides
         Finished size is 2$\frac{1}{2}$" x 19"
         Cut 2 - 3" x 19$\frac{1}{2}$"

To Assemble:

Make blocks first. Each block is made of three rows. Lay out the pieces (Fig. 1). Sew two triangles L to triangle X. Sew squares K to ends (Fig. 2). Repeat. This is top and bottom row of block.

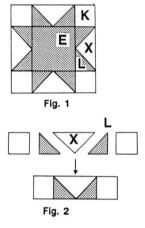

Fig. 1

Fig. 2

To make center row, sew two triangles L to triangle X (Fig. 3). Repeat. Sew these two units to either side of square E.

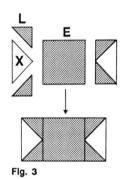

Fig. 3

Sew the three rows together (Fig. 4). Repeat to make five blocks.

Lay out pieced blocks with alternating plain blocks. Make two rows using two pieced blocks and one plain block. Make one row using one pieced block and two plain blocks. Sew blocks together to make three rows, sew rows together.

Add the borders. Sew the top and bottom inner borders. Add the top and bottom outer borders. Attach the inner side borders, then add the outer side borders. Finish the quilt following General Instructions.

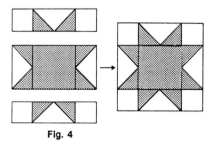

Fig. 4

Diamond in a Square

Templates to use: E, N, P

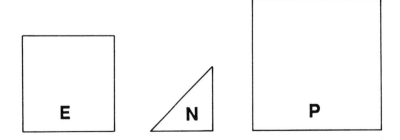

Diamond in a Square

Finished Size:
Quilt - 18$\frac{1}{4}$" x 19$\frac{1}{4}$"
($\frac{1}{2}$" binding)

Block - 2 $\frac{3}{4}$"

Number of Blocks:
13 - Pieced
12 - Plain

Number of pieces to cut:

Pieced block:

Template:	For each block:	Total:
E	1 dark or light	13
N	4 medium	52

Plain block:
P - 12

Borders:

Inner top
Finished size is 1" x 13 $\frac{3}{4}$"
Cut 1 - 1$\frac{1}{2}$" x 14$\frac{1}{4}$"

Top and bottom
Finished size is 1$\frac{3}{4}$" x 13 $\frac{3}{4}$"
Cut 2 - 2$\frac{1}{4}$" x 14$\frac{1}{4}$"

Sides
Finished size is 1$\frac{3}{4}$" x 18$\frac{1}{4}$"
Cut 2 - 2$\frac{1}{4}$" x 18 $\frac{3}{4}$"

To Assemble:

Make Pieced blocks first. Add four triangles N around square E (Fig. 1). Repeat to make 13 blocks.

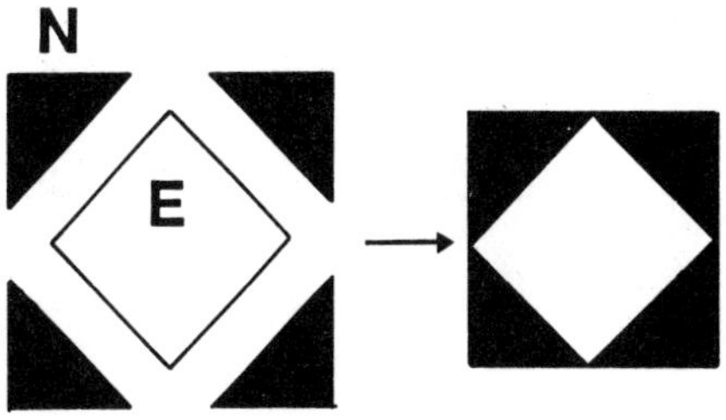

Lay out Pieced blocks and Plain blocks.

Make three rows with three Pieced blocks and two Plain blocks (Fig. 2).

Make two rows with two Pieced blocks and three Plain blocks (Fig. 3).

Sew rows together. Add the top inner border, then top and bottom border. Add the side borders. Finish the quilt following the General Instructions.

N

Fig. 1

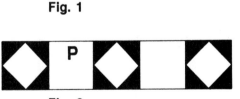

Fig. 2

Fig. 3

 **Shoo Fly**

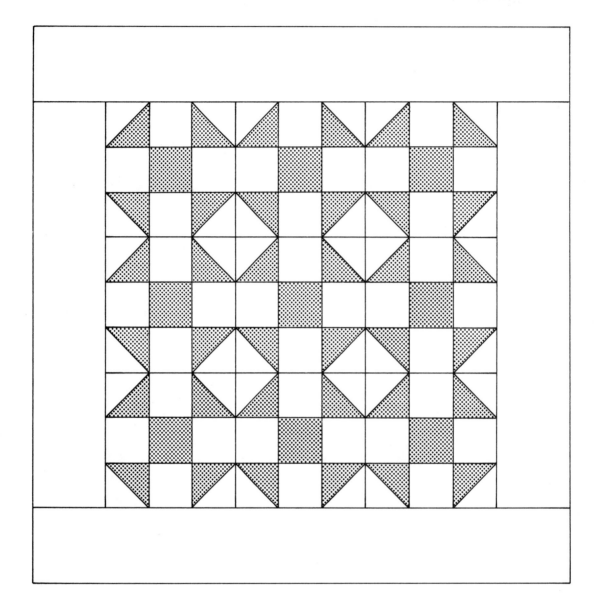

Templates to use: A, D

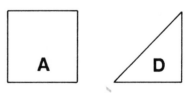

Shoo Fly

Finished Size:

Quilt - 19" x 19"
($\frac{1}{4}$" binding)

Block - 4$\frac{1}{2}$"

Number of Blocks: 9

Number of pieces to cut:

For each block:

A	1 light, 4 dark	
D	4 light, 4 dark	

Total:

9 light, 36 dark
36 light, 36 dark

Borders:

Sides
Finished size is 2$\frac{1}{2}$" x 13$\frac{1}{2}$"
Cut 2 - 3" x 14"

Top & Bottom
Finished size is 2$\frac{1}{2}$" x 18$\frac{1}{2}$"
Cut 2 - 3" x 19"

To Assemble:

Make blocks first. Sew a light and dark D together to make a square (Fig. 1). Make four of these.

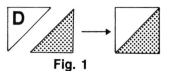

Fig. 1

Arrange the triangle-squares and squares A in rows (Fig. 2). Sew squares together to make rows (Fig. 3).

Sew rows together (Fig. 4). Repeat to make 9 blocks.

Sew three blocks together to make a row. Repeat to make three rows. Sew rows together. Add side borders, then top and bottom borders. Finish the quilt following the General Instructions.

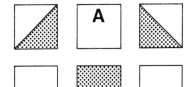

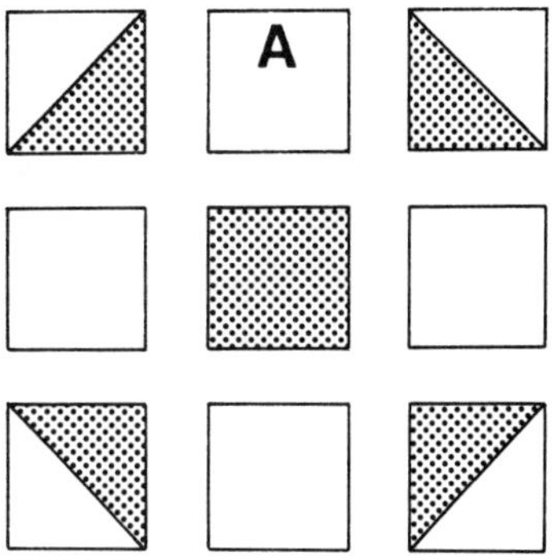

Fig. 2

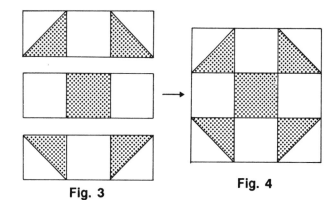

Fig. 3

Fig. 4

Shoo Fly with Lattice

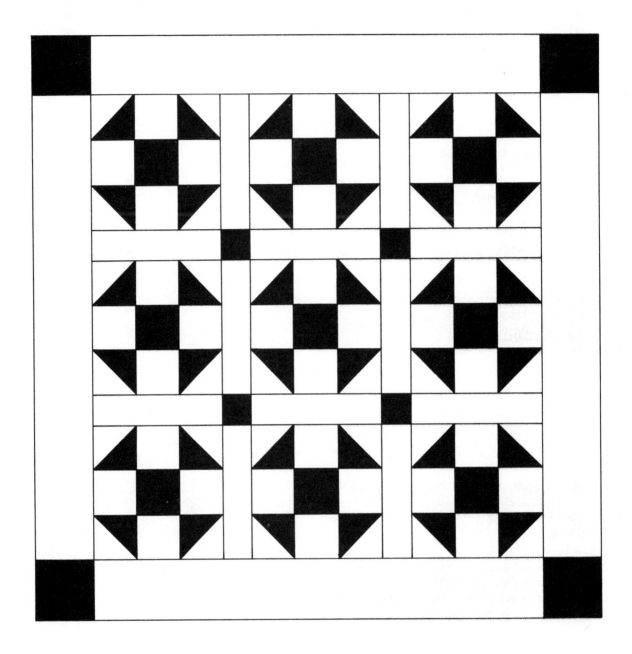

Templates to use: A, D, K, T

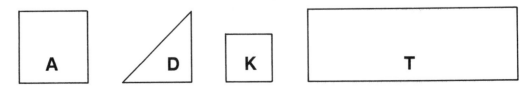

Shoo Fly with Lattice

Finished Size: **Number of Blocks: 9**

Quilt - 20" x 20"
($^1/_4$" binding)

Block - 4$^1/_2$"

Number of pieces to cut:

For each block: **Total:**   **Borders:**

Finished size is 2" x 15$^1/_2$".

A   1 dark, 4 light   9 dark, 36 light   Cut 4 - 2$^1/_2$" x 16"
D   4 dark, 4 light   36 dark, 36 light

Corner squares:
Cut 4 - 2$^1/_2$" square

Lattice:

K - 4 dark
T - 12 light

To Assemble:

Construct blocks - See Shoo Fly Quilt for
directions. Make nine blocks.

Lay out three blocks to make a row. Place a
rectangle T between the blocks. Sew blocks and
T's together to make a row (Fig. 1). Repeat to
make three rows.

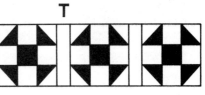

Fig. 1

Lay out three rectangles T and two squares K
(Fig. 2). Sew together, repeat to make two rows.

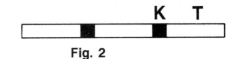

Fig. 2

Arrange block rows and lattice rows as in
drawing. Sew rows together. Add side borders.
Sew a corner square to either end of two border
pieces. Add these units to the top and bottom.
Finish the quilt following the General Instructions.

Templates to use: No templates
needed - follow cutting directions.

Bars

Finished Size:
Quilt - 21" x 21"
($^1/_2$" binding)

Number of pieces to cut:

Inner bars:
Finished size of bar is 2" x 14"
Cut bars to measure $2^1/_2$" x $14^1/_2$",
4 one color, 3 contrasting color -
7 total

Borders:
Finished size is 3" x 14"
Cut 4 - $3^1/_2$ x $14^1/_2$"

Corner squares:
Finished size is 3" square
Cut 4 - $3^1/_2$" square

To Assemble:

Sew bars together, alternating colors (Fig. 1). Add side borders. Sew corner squares to both ends of top and bottom borders. Sew these units to the top and bottom. Finish the quilt following the General Instructions.

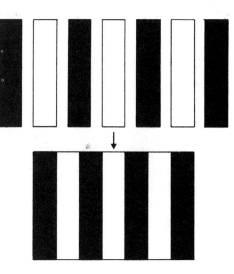

Fig. 1

Streak o' Lightning

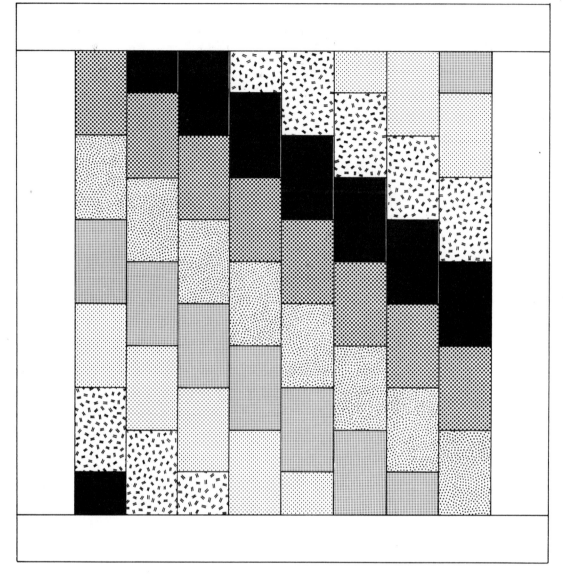

Templates to use: Y, Z

Streak o' Lightning

Finished Size:

Quilt - 19" x 19"
($^1/_2$" binding)

Number of pieces to cut:

Color	Y	Z
1	2	1
2	4	1
3	6	1
4	8	1
5	8	1
6	6	1
7	4	1
8	2	1

Borders:

Sides
Finished size is 2" x 15"
Cut 2 - $2^1/_2$" x $15^1/_2$"

Top and Bottom
Finished size is $1^1/_2$" x 18"
Cut 2 - 2" x $18^1/_2$"

To Assemble:

Following chart, lay out pieces and assemble
vertical rows A - H. Each row has five rectangles
Y and one rectangle Z. Make sure you match
the long side of Z with the short side of Y!

Sew the rows together. Add the side borders then
the top and bottom borders. Finish the quilt
following General Instructions.

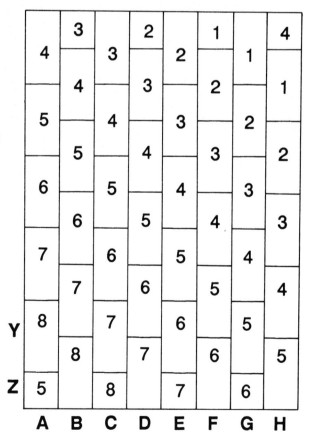

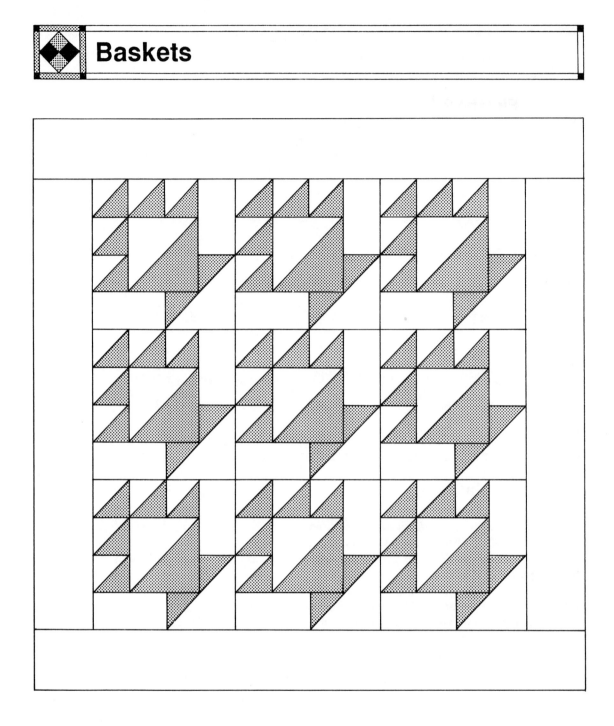

Templates to use: G, H, I

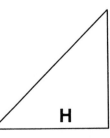

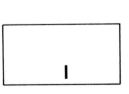

Baskets

Finished Size:

    Quilt - 19¹/₂" x 19¹/₂"
        (¹/₄" binding)

    Block - 5"

Number of Blocks: 9

Number of pieces to cut:

For each block:		Total:	Borders:
			Sides
G	7 color	63 color	Finished size is 2" x 15"
	5 black	45 black	Cut 2 - 2¹/₂" x 15¹/₂"
H	1 color	9 color	
	2 black	18 black	Top & Bottom
I	2 black	18 black	Finished size is 2" x 19"
			Cut 2 - 2¹/₂" x 19¹/₂"

To Assemble:

Make the blocks first.

1. Make five "square units" from black (background) and color triangles G (Fig. 1).

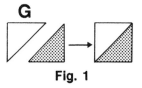

G

Fig. 1

Sew three "square units" together to form a row (Fig. 2).

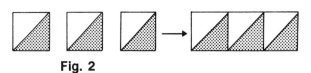

Fig. 2

Sew two "square units" together to form a column (Fig. 3).

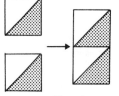

Fig. 3

Sew a black (background) triangle H to a color H to make a large square (Fig. 4).

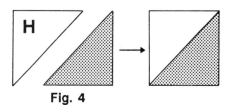

H

Fig. 4

Baskets

2. Sew the column to one side (Fig. 5).

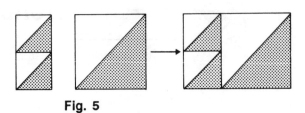

Fig. 5

3. Sew the row on top (Fig. 6).

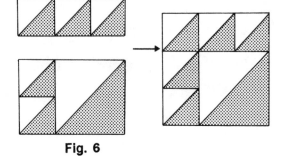

Fig. 6

4. Sew a color triangle G to one end of rectangle I. Repeat, making sure triangle G is in the correct orientation (Fig. 7).

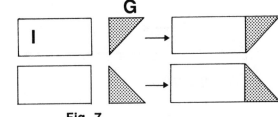

Fig. 7

5. Sew G-I units to the sides of the large square. Add a background triangle H (Fig. 8).

Repeat to make nine blocks. Lay out the blocks following the drawing. Sew the blocks together to make three rows, then sew the rows together.

Add the side borders, then the top and bottom borders.

Finish the quilt following the General Instructions.

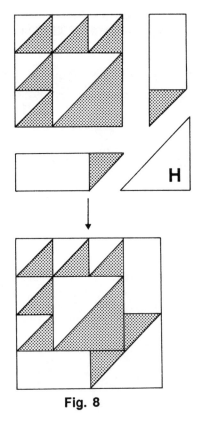

Fig. 8

Monkey Wrench

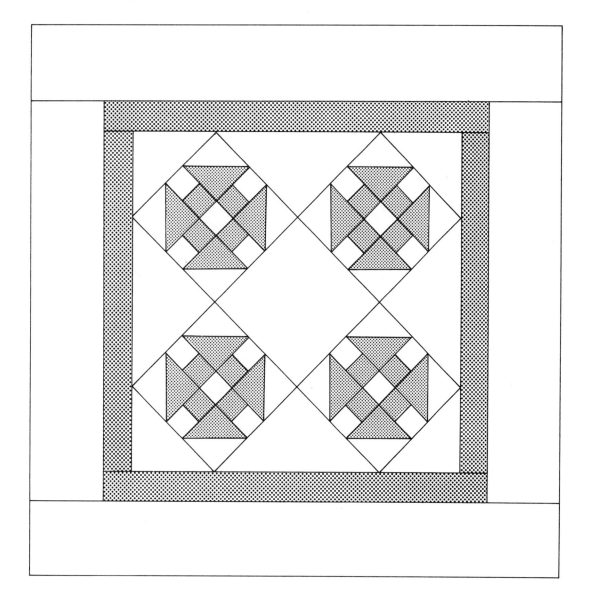

Templates to use:

MW - 1, 2, 3, 4

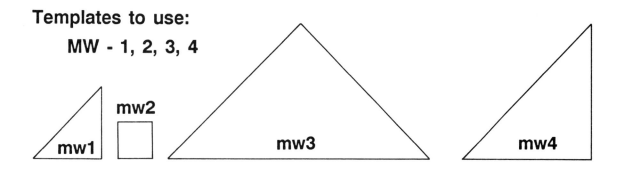

mw2

mw1

mw3

mw4

Monkey Wrench

Finished Size: **Number of Blocks: 4**

Quilt - 19" x 19"
($\frac{1}{4}$" binding)

Block - 4"

Number of pieces to cut:

For each block:		Total:
MW 1	4 light	16 light
	4 dark	16 dark
MW 2	4 light	16 light
	5 dark	20 dark

(lights can be all the same or
different for each block)

From dark (background):
Cut one $4\frac{1}{2}$" square for center
MW 3 - cut 4
MW 4 - cut 4

Borders:

Inner   Sides
Finished size is 1" x $11\frac{1}{2}$"
Cut 2 - $1\frac{1}{2}$" x 12"

Top and bottom
Finished size is 1" x $13\frac{1}{2}$"
Cut 2 - $1\frac{1}{2}$" x 14"

Outer   Sides
Finished size is $2\frac{1}{2}$" x $13\frac{1}{2}$"
Cut 2 - 3" x 14"

Top and bottom
Finished size is $2\frac{1}{2}$" x $18\frac{1}{2}$"
Cut 2 - 3" x 19"

To Assemble:

Make blocks first.
Sew a light triangle 1 to a dark triangle 1 (Row 1,
Fig. 1). Repeat.

Sew a light square 2 to a dark square 2 (Row 1,
Fig. 1).

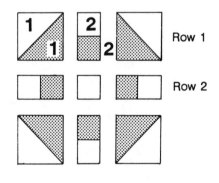

Fig. 1

46

Monkey Wrench

Sew the triangle-square units to the square unit (Row 1, Fig. 2). Make two of these rows.

Make two more of the square 2 units (Row 2, Fig. 1). Sew these together with a light square 2 in the middle (Row 2, Fig. 2).

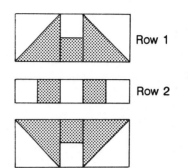

Fig. 2

Sew these three rows together (Fig. 3). Repeat to make four blocks.

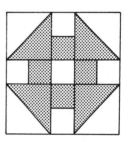

Fig. 3

Lay out the Monkey Wrench blocks, center square, set-in triangles 3, and corner triangles 4 (Fig. 4). Construct the quilt in diagonal rows (Row 1, Row 2, Row 3 - Fig. 4). Sew the blocks and triangles together to make the rows. Sew the rows together, then add the last two corner triangles.

Add the borders. Sew the inner side borders to the quilt, then add the top and bottom inner borders. Attach the outer side borders, then add the outer top and bottom borders. Finish quilt following the General Instructions.

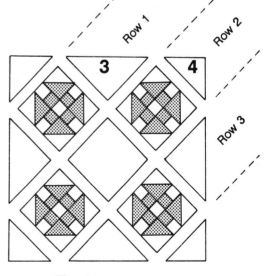

Fig. 4